Georgia's
Location and
Resources

Wendy Conklin, M.A.

Consultants

Regina Holland, Ed.S., *Henry County Schools*
Christina Noblet, Ed.S., *Paulding County*
School District
Jennifer Troyer, *Paulding County Schools*

Publishing Credits

Rachelle Cracchiolo, M.S.Ed., *Publisher*
Conni Medina, M.A.Ed., *Managing Editor*
Emily R. Smith, M.A.Ed., *Series Developer*
Diana Kenney, M.A.Ed., NBCT, *Content Director*
Torrey Maloof, *Editor*
Courtney Patterson, *Multimedia Designer*

Image Credits: Cover: DEA/V. CORDIOLI/De Agostini/
Getty Images; pp. 3,9 Philip Scalia/Alamy; p. 4 Joe Vogan/
Alamy; p. 8 Wang Lei Xinhua News Agency/Newscom;
p. 14 Courtesy of the Thomaston-Upson Archives; p. 17
(left) Public Domain, (right) Sean Pavone/Alamy; p. 20
Margaret Bourke-White/The LIFE Picture Collection/Getty
Images; p. 23 Paras Griffin/Getty Images; All other images
from Shutterstock and iStock.

Library of Congress Cataloging-in-Publication Data

Names: Conklin, Wendy, author.
Title: Georgia's location and resources / Wendy Conklin.
Description: Huntington Beach, CA : Teacher Created
Materials, 2016. |
  Includes index.
Identifiers: LCCN 2015042450 | ISBN 9781493825493
(pbk.)
Subjects: LCSH: Georgia--Juvenile literature. | Georgia--
Geography--Juvenile
  literature. | Georgia--Economic conditions--Juvenile
literature. | Natural
  resources--Georgia--Juvenile literature. | Industries--
Georgia--Juvenile
  literature.
Classification: LCC F286.3 .C66 2016 | DDC 975.8--dc23
LC record available at http://lccn.loc.gov/2015042450

Teacher Created Materials

5301 Oceanus Drive
Huntington Beach, CA 92649-1030
http://www.tcmpub.com
ISBN 978-1-4938-2549-3
© 2017 Teacher Created Materials, Inc.
Printed in China
Nordica.072018.CA21800844

Table of Contents

How You Live

People live in different places. Some live in cities. Some live in **rural** areas. Others live in **suburbs**. Where you live tells people about you. It may tell where your family is from. It may tell what is important to you. It may tell what needs you have. It definitely affects *how* you live.

How you live depends on the resources available. If there is only one store in a small town, the shopping choices are limited. If people need more choices, they move to a different place.

What places are there to live in Georgia?

Small Town

The world's largest peanut is in the small town of Ashburn. But the peanut is really a sculpture.

GEORGIA 1ST *In* PEANUTS

Atlanta, Georgia

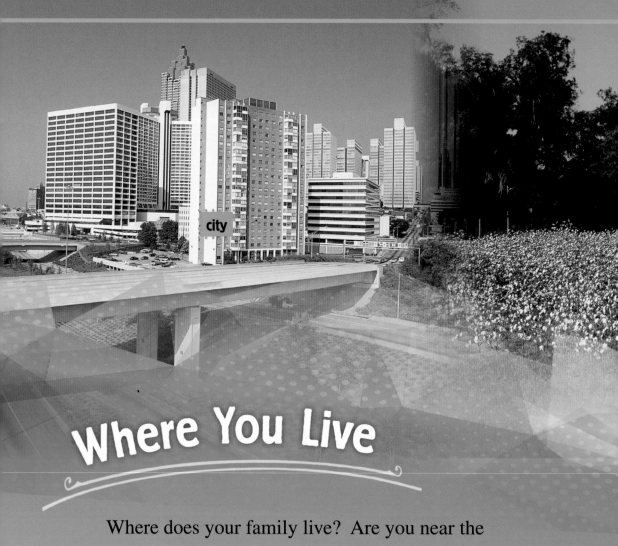

city

Where You Live

Where does your family live? Are you near the beach? Some families have farms. Others live in busy cities.

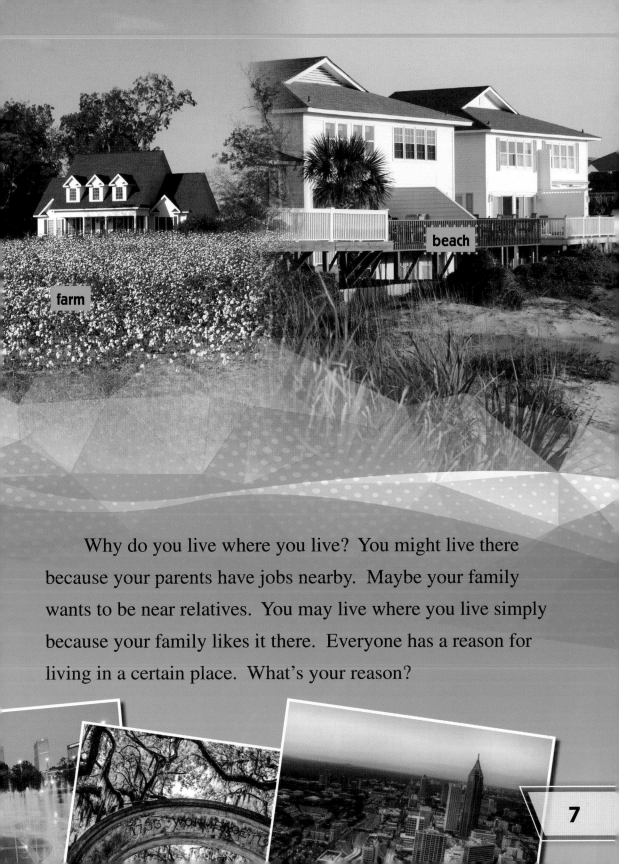

farm

beach

Why do you live where you live? You might live there
because your parents have jobs nearby. Maybe your family
wants to be near relatives. You may live where you live simply
because your family likes it there. Everyone has a reason for
living in a certain place. What's your reason?

Living in the City

Georgia has many places to live. Do you hear honking car horns and buses as they rush by? Do the streetlights glow at night? Are there many stores to choose from when you need to buy things? If this is true for you, then you likely live in a city. Atlanta is a city in Georgia.

You can do many things in the city of Atlanta. It has one of the biggest **aquariums** in the world! You can see giant pandas at Zoo Atlanta. You can even go to Piedmont (PEED-mahnt) Park. A famous artist created a playground there that looks like a work of art!

giant pandas

Parks Change

Long ago, Piedmont Park had a Ferris wheel and a water slide. Now, it has a playground and bike trails.

Piedmont Park

Living on a Farm

Have you ever tasted peach cobbler? Yum! The peaches in that dessert might have come from a Georgia farm.

There are over 40,000 farms in the state! They grow **crops** such as cotton and peanuts. The sweetest onion in the world grows here. It is called the Vidalia (vuh-DAYL-yuh) onion. But Georgia farms not only grow crops. There are chicken farms, too.

If you live on a farm in the state, you may have chores. You may take care of animals. You may help **harvest** crops.

Onion Law

Only 20 counties in Georgia can grow Vidalia onions. It's the law! They need just the right soil.

cotton

peanuts

peaches

Living on the Coast

Can you taste the salt in the air? Can you feel the sand between your toes? Welcome to the Georgia coast! While visiting the beach, you can swim, boat, or fish. Many people go to the beaches on Jekyll Island. There are **dunes** where you can run and play.

You can stay in a beach house or a hotel. But some people live here all the time. Many fishermen live along the beaches. They catch fish and sell them at the markets. They also ship their fish all over the world!

A man uses a net to catch fish.

A Long Shore

Georgia has 100 miles of shoreline! It is where the land meets the water.

Resources

Georgia is important! It has **products** that other places want. Long ago, cotton was the largest crop. Now, more peanuts and pecans are grown there than in any other state.

Crops are not the only products made in the state. People make carpets. They also make soft drinks, paper, and airplanes. They mine **granite** there, too. People use granite in their homes. People who live far away like to eat shrimp and shellfish from the state, too. Even the pine trees grown there help make **rosin** (RAHZ-ihn). It is used in gum, glue, and soap.

Carpet factory workers inspect a roll of cotton in the 1950s.

granite mine

Making Products

Have you ever wondered how the things we buy get to the stores? It's not a magic trick!

Coca-Cola® is made in Georgia. But how does this drink get into grocery stores? First, the recipe for this soft drink is mixed in a factory. Then, the drink is bottled. It is shipped to stores in trucks. When we go shopping, we can buy it.

Georgia stores have many great things to buy. But there are some things you will not find there.

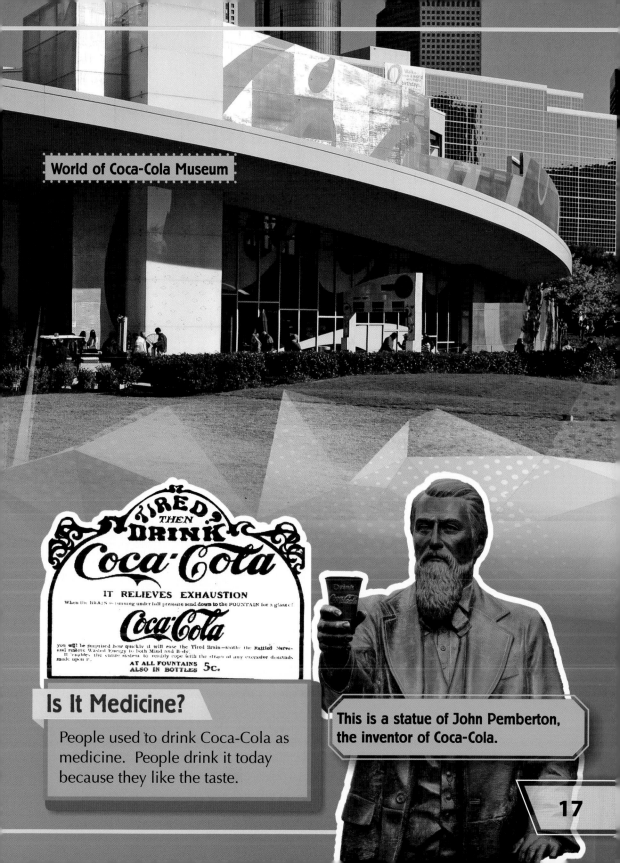

World of Coca-Cola Museum

TIRED? THEN DRINK Coca-Cola

IT RELIEVES EXHAUSTION

When the BRAIN is running under full pressure send down to the FOUNTAIN for a glass of

Coca-Cola

you will be surprised how quickly it will ease the Tired Brain—soothe the Rattled Nerves and restore Wasted Energy to both Mind and Body. It enables the entire system to readily cope with the strain of any excessive demands made upon it.

AT ALL FOUNTAINS ALSO IN BOTTLES 5c.

Is It Medicine?

People used to drink Coca-Cola as medicine. People drink it today because they like the taste.

This is a statue of John Pemberton, the inventor of Coca-Cola.

17

Products are shipped on boats from the port of Savannah.

Shipping Products

You will have a hard time finding snow shovels for sale in Georgia. Why? Because it does not snow very often there. Stores carry products that people will buy. Store owners are smart. They don't sell items that no one wants or needs.

Go shopping and you will find plenty of products made in Georgia. You will also find things not made in the state. Let's say you want a pair of jeans. How do the jeans get to Georgia? Products from other places get there the same way the state gets its products to other places. They are shipped on trucks, boats, and planes.

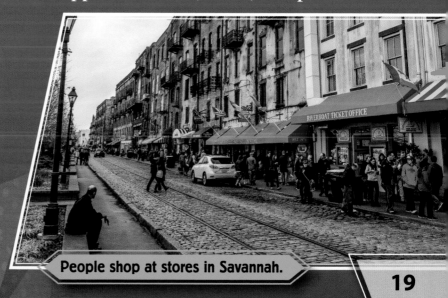

People shop at stores in Savannah.

What's Available?

Let's say you really want the latest action figure. You go to the toy store to buy it. But you see a sign. It says, "Sold out!"

In 1939, this small store had limited items for sale.

If you live in a city, you might be able to find the toy at another store. If you live in a rural place where there are not many stores, you may not be so lucky. You may need to wait until the store gets more. Or you may order it online and have it shipped to your home.

Today, Savannah has many stores that sell what people want.

Cost

Have you ever wondered why some things cost more where you live than other things? In Georgia, two different kinds of peaches may be on the shelf. The Georgia peaches cost less than the Texas peaches. Peaches from Texas are smaller but cost more. Why?

One peach may be cheaper because it is grown in the state where it is sold. It does not have to travel far to reach the stores, so it does not cost as much.

At times, an item costs more because everyone wants it. This means the value of the item is higher. Store owners know what buyers want. They can make the prices high because they know it will sell.

The Texas peach travels farther, which raises its cost.

$1.00

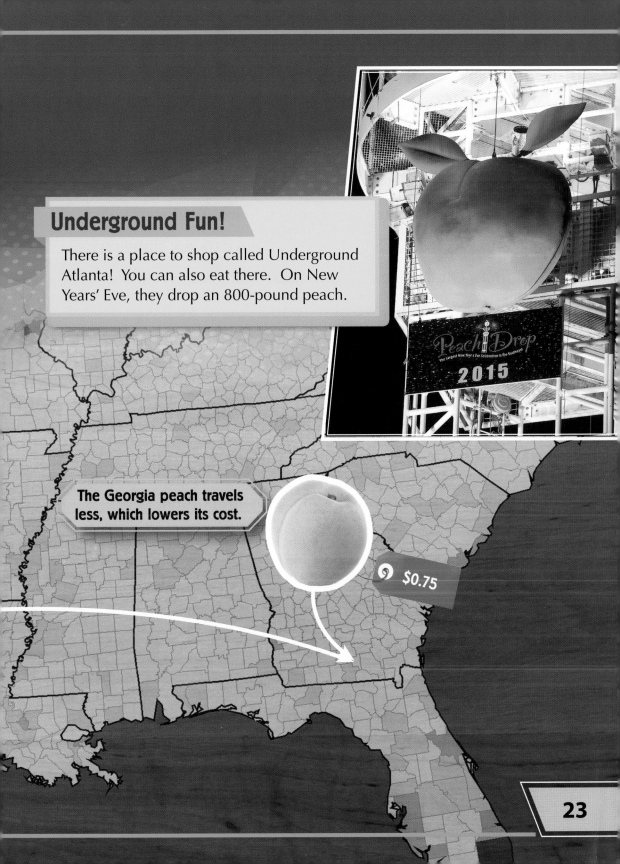

Underground Fun!

There is a place to shop called Underground Atlanta! You can also eat there. On New Years' Eve, they drop an 800-pound peach.

Peach Drop
The Largest New Year's Eve Celebration in the Southeast
2015

The Georgia peach travels less, which lowers its cost.

$0.75

Choices

Sometimes we have to make choices. We cannot have everything we want. Sometimes we have to buy things we need first. Other times, we have to think about what we want the most. Then, we have to make sure we have enough money to pay for the items.

This not only applies to our money. It also applies to our time. Think about your school day. Your teacher makes choices about what is most important to learn. He or she makes a schedule. That schedule helps you learn the most important things first. That is how you stay on track.

Needs	Wants
Food	toys
Water	video games
clothes	books
medicine	movies

Loving Life in Georgia

There are many places to live in Georgia. Some people work and live near the beach. Others farm the land and grow tasty crops. And some live in big cities where there are many different things to do.

Where you live affects *how* you live. It makes a difference in the job you have, the things you buy, and the choices you make. Location and resources go hand in hand.

Downtown Atlanta

Blue Mountains

Look at the Blue Ridge Mountains on a misty day. They really do look blue!

Choose It!

Think of two places you might live in Georgia. Think about the resources that are available to people in each place. Make a list of pros and cons for each of the two places. Pros tell all the things you like about that place. Cons tell the things you don't like about that place. Then, use the list to help you choose which place is best for you!

Pros | Cons

Glossary

aquariums—buildings people visit to see water, animals, and plants

crops—groups of plants grown by farmers

dunes—hills of sand near the ocean or desert that form by wind

factory—a building where products are made

granite—a very hard rock that is used in monuments, buildings, and homes

harvest—to gather or collect a crop

products—things that are made or grown to be sold or used

rosin—a hard, sticky substance that comes from pine trees and is used to make many things

rural—relating to the country or area outside a town or city

suburbs—towns where people live that are near cities

Index

Your Turn!

Many Resources

Where you live plays a part in what you eat, what you do for fun, and how you spend your money. Think about how the resources where you live are different from the resources in other places. Create a chart that shows people all the wonderful things your town has to offer.